Aw Sl

Dear Mom: War

What's the point anyway?

It's not true. It's not false. It's all just an experiment. Providing a safe space to fail freely.

*A book of my thoughts, essays, prose, and poems.
What's the point anyway?*

By: LaTanya M Coleman-Carter

CONTENTS

Acknowledgments 1

Preface 2

Part One 4

This is Absurd 5

Grits with cheese 8

Normal Isn't For Everyone: How My Son Taught
Me a Lesson in Schooling 12

Free? 16

Part Two 18

Trick or Treat 19

Timeout 21

Don't Choke, wait... 26

Dear Performing Arts Magnet, 28

I don't want to work for you and my kids don't either. 32

Finding Your Path: My Gamer Son Played Your Test 34

Part Three 39

Why you got that attitude?!? 40

One thing I know; two things for certain 46

Wait, Am I doing this right?   49

Just Imagine   52

Wrecking Ball   55

What's your name?   65

Go see it for yourself   68

To be or not to be... Humble   71

Humpty Dumpty   74

I didn't ask to be born.   77

PS   82
Playlist   83

Acknowledgments

To my kids, who allowed me to use their experiences to tell a story and have forgiven me over and over 'cause I had no idea what I was doing.

To my partner, who no matter what reminded me that this project is a "big deal!" I've wanted to write a book for years, and now I get to check it off my list. You're right, it's a big deal. You were the first person to tell me to tell the story. You've believed in me for a very long time. Thanks for the continued support and encouragement.

To my mother, who is my inspiration. I learned it all from watching you. You showed me exactly what it looks like to advocate and support my kids. I am so thankful to have had such an amazing example. I honestly hope that I have made you proud and that I continue to do so.

My amazing editors, I'm forever thankful. It's so helpful to have you all in my corner. My first language is AAVE, and it's often hard for me to translate, but you all understood and know my voice. You all also appreciate the art of my being and were open to me keeping some necessary "improper" English.

I truly have some of the best friends. Thank you for welcoming my weirdness and encouraging me to share. I've bounced a million ideas off you. I really appreciate the "hell yeahs" and "what the fucks" over tea and cognac!

Song: *"Legacy"* - Jay-Z

Preface

I'm weird. Wait, am I weird? They said I was weird. Who are they? Where do I start? So many people have said that to me. It's now weird when someone doesn't think I'm weird. Weird huh? See.

This book is my weird. It's sporadic. It's my thoughts on paper. It's a book about how I've decided to parent my children. So, it defies rules and may not seem to make sense. It's mostly written in my native tongue of AAVE along with my take on absurdism. I speak with the goal of communicating.

My family and I love to paint. I definitely enjoy the freedom that it gives me, especially with oil paints because they allow me to move the paint around the canvas. One of my favorite things about painting is that there's no way to make a mistake. It's art. Even when I've made what I thought was a mistake, I'm always pleased with how it turned out because it never really was a mistake at all.

I see art in everything. I love all art forms. I know that the arts are equally as important as math and science. So, it only made sense for me to incorporate some of my art and a playlist of music that enhances the emotion behind each piece. Most of the art pieces were previously painted. A few were created specifically for the book. The playlist has some of my favorite artists included.

My hope is that by adding some of the paintings from my art collection, it helps give you a visual for my words. My intention is that you get a full experience. I have also included a mixtape (playlist). It is so natural for me to create a playlist for the book because I have so many on my phone. I pretty much make one for every thing, every emotion, every situation, every type of party. Music is one of the things that has the ability to change me emotionally. The songs chosen here are songs I've previously heard. After I wrote the book, I felt they fit each piece the best.

Part One

This is Absurd

I parent differently
because the world is different.

The *WORLD* isn't different.

The world IS different.

I was a teenage mom. I was still a kid.

My first kid grew up with me.

We discovered things together.

I became the mom I was told I should be.

Society showed me.

TV *taught* me. Religion *cursed* me.

With

all

this
education

I still was unknowing.

I wasn't always the parent I am now.

The parent I was, died. It was a slow death.

It was a necessary
DEATH.

All endings are new beginnings.

Song: *"A Change is Gonna Come"* - Sam Cooke

This is Absurd, 2021, Acrylic

Grits with cheese

The realization that traditional school is failing some of my own children, and probably my community, led me to this dream.

My family had moved to Los Angeles from Little Rock, Arkansas to give in-state tuition to my oldest daughter. The rise of her life achievement was the fall of my career. Prior to the move, I had been a professor of mathematics and even tried my hand in teaching middle and high school at a charter school in Arkansas.

After we arrived in Los Angeles, I was unable to secure employment, which led me to tutor professionally. More importantly, I became a homemaker with four of our children living in the home.

In the role of homemaker, I became more vigilant in the interest of my children, beyond my personal desires, to have them all become traditionally high achieving students. An idea I know stemmed from my personal experiences in the society we live in. I had been successful thus far as my oldest had excelled academically from hard work, dedication, and grit. Watching her apply to top schools and be accepted had proven to me that my methods were a recipe for success.

Hard work, dedication, and grit is all it takes, right? So, why was my now 12 year old struggling with the very thing I had proven possible? The truth is that she wasn't struggling at all. She possessed all of those very qualities. They looked different, and I almost missed it. It was not academically visible (at least not in the traditional sense). I pondered what I had done wrong, and why I was unable to reach her the same way I did my oldest. I recalled the time she wanted to learn gymnastics. I couldn't afford classes, so she took it upon herself to learn via YouTube. I was completely impressed when she showed me her back handspring. She continued in her efforts to learn in this matter never asking for anything from me (good thing because I had never taken gymnastics), until the day she wanted to learn how to do a no hand cartwheel. She asked if I would purchase a gymnastics mat because we had hardwood floors, and she was certain she would fall several times in her practice. She had even gone as far as looking on Amazon and finding the cheapest mat. This too was hard work, dedication, and grit. Unfortunately for her, this is not what comes across in her school environment and therefore, she is told the very opposite about herself.

It's not enough to say grit is what is missing from students in the school system. I believe we have to go further in seeing that this said "grit" may look different for each student. Once we find the grit for the individual student, it should become a part of the curriculum. General skills needed in life can be taught through the interest of the child.

Song: *"Ready or Not"* - Fugees

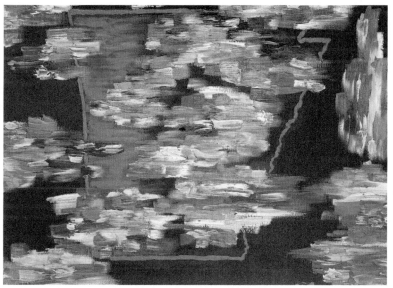

Grit with Cheese, 2021, Oil

Normal Isn't For Everyone: How My Son Taught Me a Lesson in Schooling

A story about why I started homeschooling my 8 year old son: reason number one.

It's time for his annual physical, and my son couldn't care less. He enters the exam room with a slow stride and blue mohawk and sits down on the white paper covered patient table. The doctor asks if he is eating his fruits and vegetables. He says, "a little" and without fail, she then asks, "Don't you want to be a big, strong, tall man?" Again without fail, he says, "No." Well damn!

That is my son in a nutshell. He has stayed clear of societal norms. It is so normal to hear that men should be strong for so many different reasons: to survive, to thrive, to work, to get the money, or to get the girl. He does not care what normal is, and it is one of my favorite things about him. Herein lies one of the reasons I started homeschooling him.

My son has absolutely hated school since kindergarten. I completely understood why. His classroom had none of the centers we remember: a reading center, home center, or blocks. There were no naps. No joy. Just straight to the seriousness of school.

Every morning he would cry when I woke him. He would cry the entire time he got dressed. The whole ride to school and as he walked in the gate. It was heartbreaking to watch. Other parents thought he was my first child. They would offer their two cents: "He will stop crying when he gets inside the class," "he will only do this the first week," and many more cliché statements. But this wasn't my first child. I was aware of the things they said, but this was not that. He hated school.

To add insult to injury, every year his teachers told me that he was behind and that he needed intervention (additional after-school help) to help get him on par with his cohort. He was a quiet kid and didn't get excited about things that didn't interest him. He wouldn't finish the assigned work and daydreamed about playing video games. As a July baby, he's a year younger than most of the kids he was being compared to in class. When teachers told me during parent-teacher conferences that he was behind, I always told them that to better assess him, they need to stop comparing him to his peers and only compare him to himself. Was he learning? Does he know more now than he knew last year? Does he know more now than he did at the beginning of this school year?

Teachers always made it known to my son that he was behind by posting the achievements in the classroom. They even went as far as having an assembly to acknowledge how great other kids were doing. They argued that the purpose was to motivate the other students. This is not motivation for him, nor do I agree with this process.

So, I had to ask myself, why am I forcing him to do something he hates? What kind of world forces people to do things they hate? I thought I should simply move him to a different school. Maybe he didn't hate school, maybe he hated that particular school. Around this time, I had also noticed that he was spending a lot of time on his Xbox. I found a STEAM (Education is an approach to learning that uses Science, Technology, Engineering, the Arts and

Mathematics) magnet school that offered robotics and legos as part of the curriculum. I thought this school may spark an interest for learning within a school setting because by then, I knew my son didn't mind learning. Clearly, he has the capacity to learn what interests him because he masters each new game I buy faster than I can replace them. I was hoping that a school with a STEAM focus would do the trick. He still hated it!

TO BE CONTINUED...

Song: *"Liberation"*- Outkast

Normal isn't for Everyone, 2019, Oil

Free?

What's Free...are we really FREE?

Are we free to be who we are?

How can we know?

I would like to make one thing very clear before I start: I am
no expert.

I don't even pretend to know what I am doing,
and I understand that life is an experiment
and that no one can tell you how to do any part of it.

There are some choices I still make for my children.

How free am I willing to let them be?
Do they know that they are free?
Does it make a difference...if they don't think they are free,
but I know I've given freedom?

Are they still free?

Are you free because you have freedom?

The definition of free is not the same for everyone

Song: "*What's Free*"- Meek Mill

Free, 2021, Acrylic

Part Two

Trick or Treat

We have all been told how important it is to read.

Most families have that one kid who loves to read.

Parents threaten to take away their child's books as a punishment.

Yeah I didn't get one of those.

All mine hate to read.

I hate making people do things they don't want to do.

But I actually agree that reading is important.

I trick them into reading.

I told them to put the closed captions on their devices.

So as they watch Netflix, YouTube, or whatever, the words will be there.

Whether they know it or not they are reading.

Or at least seeing the words as they are being said.

It's a trick. Some call it a hack.

Song: "*Neighbors*"- J. Cole

Trick or Treat, 2021, Acrylic

Timeout

A running theme in my parenting is that all my kids are different. It is necessary that you understand that I love this about them and our house. Can you imagine having the same child four times? Boring!

I have not quite figured my youngest out. It seems to me that she is a combination of all of the ones that came before her. I usually say she is a sponge; she absorbs trace amounts of every environment, situation, and person she encounters. She takes what she needs and leaves the rest. Sort of like at the grocery store when you pick your apples. There are lots of good apples, but you don't need them all. She is smart, intellectual, and creative. She likes to learn and explore, but she will also dance and play video games. She does all of these things really well.

My youngest is also very observant. She noticed really early on (when she was about four) that the kids in school who simply "did what the teacher asked and followed the rules, had it easier" (these were her words on the way home from school one day). She did not necessarily agree with the school rules, but she had factored the results of just following them so that she could obtain the easiest end result.

She went through an entire school year unscathed. No blemishes on her record. So, you can imagine my surprise when she gets in the car after school one kindergarten day and says, "Mom, I got put in timeout today." My initial response, "OMG baby, I am so proud of you!" She was shocked. She expected me to be angry or disappointed. This is what the school and her teacher led her to believe my reaction to a timeout would be. On the contrary, I was pleased and happy to see that she had stepped out of the box. She never gets timeout. I mean, the fact that she had possibly done something she wanted even though it was against the rule or unfavorably looked on; like damn, I'm wit it! She was so confused by my response that she told me that I was not supposed to be happy that my kid got in timeout. She asked why would I be happy that she did a bad thing. I realized she was right, maybe I should find out exactly what she did before I saw it as a victory. I asked what she did. She went to timeout because her stomach was hurting. I found this hard to believe. I thought surely she misunderstood, so I contacted the teacher. She confirmed and went even further to say, "her stomach hurts everyday." She had the audacity to go on to say that her stomach hurts everyday at the same time, which happened to be after lunch. She put her in timeout because she wanted to let her know it was not okay to lie in an effort to get out of doing her work. First of all, that is not a reason to put someone in timeout. Secondly, she has Hirschsprung's disease, which was documented at enrollment. Hirschsprung's disease is a digestive disease, and one symptom is stomach pain. So, it turned out that my child was not taking a risk at all. She was actually being punished because her teacher did not take the time to read the enrollment information, which would have told her a little more about the student.

I explained to my child that the teacher's actions were inappropriate. I went one step further to say that adults are not always right. I also explained to her that my excitement about her timeout had everything to do with the idea of seeing her take risks and explore her desires in a world that is so controlling. I told her that I trusted her, and I knew that if she had made the decision, she had properly calculated the risk and consequences.

Imagine my child coming home with a disciplinary slip needing my signature for proof that I was made aware of her being put in timeout. Then, imagine me simply punishing her for getting in trouble with the teacher. My view on punishment is so different from most of the world. I don't believe that just because someone thinks certain actions are punishable, I should.

At this age, my first daughter walked the straight and narrow, the middle daughter was the riskiest person I had ever met, my son was the calmest, and somehow my youngest daughter found the middle ground. She is a sponge.

Song: *"This Is America"*- Childish Gambino

Time Out, 2021, Acrylic

Don't Choke, wait...

Do I make everything about race?
IS everything about race?
You made me feel a way.
You made me feel this way.
You! Not YOU.

I'm not trying to hide. Look at me.
I am black. I can't hide. I embrace it.
I talk about race. I have to. I am race.
Race was created because I exist.

Go deeper. Go inward.
The answer is there.
I did. I do.
Inward is Blacker. My ancestors are there.

You say "don't let it stress you". It don't stress me. You are
stressed.
You hear my life and it stresses you. I live this shit. I'm not
stressed, it's normal.
It stresses you to hear my normal.

Are you uncomfortable? Do I make you uncomfortable?
I love being black.
I will continue to talk race as long as race is on every
application.
To pretend it doesn't exist is the antithesis of my existence.
I'm not interested in being palatable.
You can choke.

Song: "I'm Black" - Styles P

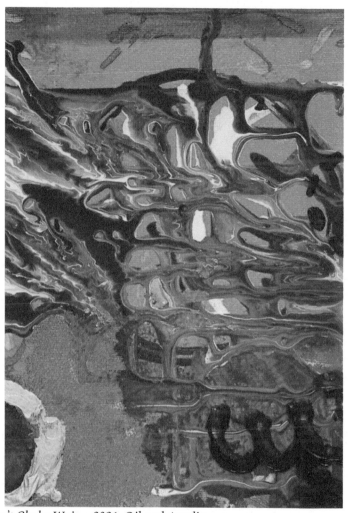

Don't Choke Wait..., 2021, Oil and Acrylic

Dear Performing Arts Magnet,

You have been a complete disappointment to my daughter and me. Why do you call yourself a performing arts school if you provide a little more than every other public school? We thought your school would be exactly what we had figured out our creatively talented 13-year old daughter needed. We thought (based on your name) that your school would be an environment that understands creativity; a place that understands that some minds/thought processes are different, and that's not "bad"; a place that would not judge solely from a piece of paper (report card), but would see the whole person. All in all, a place that viewed the arts as equally important as STEM.

Our daughter loves to perform in any capacity that allows her to express herself. Most often it's through dance, and she does not hold back simply because it's not allowed at the moment. We've always known that she is a naturally gifted performer. What we did not know was that she needed a school to support and nurture her personality type. We knew she was different but didn't know how much trouble it would cause in a traditional school; we didn't know she was "special needs." We wanted to find a better option to traditional schools that punished her for being different. We were thrilled to find a school that we perceived to be a place (based on the name) that hones and encourages her energy and love for dance, while also having teachers and administrators who would understand and appreciate her personality and overwhelming desire to perform. But, you have failed me and my daughter.

I was hoping you would help me help her by actually doing what you said in your mission statement, but you have been drinking the same Kool-Aid as every other basic and uninspiring public school. She has endured and been unnecessarily subjected to a curriculum focused heavily on traditional subject matters, without offering options for different learning styles and demeaning rebukes for not learning traditionally. Even more so, she has had to be on the wrong side of a system where students are rewarded based on academics and "good behavior,"and a heavy handed administration punishes every and all offenses while still emotionally attached to an antiquated "19th century" standard of schools. Instead of being a place of learning that understands her unique personality and allows her to explore her artform, you trampled her creative energy, condemned her free spirit, and crushed her excitement for a change from the status quo. What is the point of including "performing arts" in the title of your school? It is misleading to students and parents who think it is a place where kids are to be artsy and carefree.

Providing the same type of education as any other public school restricts the development of creative students. I know you must adhere to a particular curriculum as outlined by the state of California, but your efforts to ensure my daughter is exposed to the arts, just as much as she is to math and other traditional subjects, is unacceptable. You simply provided additional options for electives but did not operate from a space of recognizing why that was necessary to do. We were clearly misled by the title and the expectation of change, but you made it very clear, fairly early on, that you had the right idea but were unable to fully execute.

However, I am not giving up because I cannot for my child's sake. I offered to homeschool her, but she feels she will miss out on the social experience of being at school. So I will try again - at a "performing arts" high school - in hopes that this time the name might actually mean something; she needs this to work. I feel that she needs this to work because, ultimately, I do not want her to give up on her craft or herself. I definitely feel like it is our responsibility, as a society, to let her feel the importance of what she does now and not wait until she is old enough for you to pay to see her perform. We have to recognize that we enjoy the arts as adults, and it's an important part of one's life experience. These artists are not made, they were born this way.

Sincerely,
Concerned Parent

Song: "Mad"- Solange

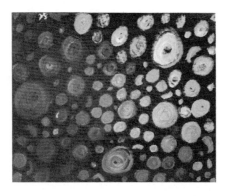

Dear Performing Arts, 2017, Oil

I don't want to work for you and my kids don't either.

Have schools and institutions even asked employers what they are looking for?

Why has school/education remained unchanged in its delivery?

Employers want people to help create solutions.

Not a "what do you need me to do, boss" person.

This is not the industrial age.

This is not the internet age.

This is the creative age.

Get creative.

Or

Get Left.

Song: *"Shelfless"*- The Clew

I don't want to work for you and my kids don't either, 2021, Acrylic

Finding Your Path: My Gamer Son Played Your Test

A story about why I started homeschooling my 8 year old son continued: reason number two

After noticing my son's love of video games, I thought I would find a STEAM school that would embrace his interest in gaming in order to help him learn within a school setting. I had no luck. This new school was better. My son still hated the regimented approach to learning that a school encourages. So, I spent a summer learning more about gaming and its future in the world. I read tons of articles and watched a lot of youtube videos. I also spent time watching him play the games he loved. I asked him lots of questions in an effort to gain a more in-depth understanding of what appealed to him. The most important thing I learned about gaming was that my then 8 year old son was an exceptional gamer, which requires skills and knowledge that were not fully exploited or understood by traditional schools. I also learned that gaming is a lucrative business in which he could have a fulfilling career. I became very comfortable with gaming being his primary focus.

It was not easy for me to change my thinking about what an education should entail for my son. Everything I had ever been told about gaming suggested it was bad for his learning and his social skills. I had to free myself from that idea in order to figure out how to translate my son's interests into activities that would continue to nurture and improve his skills. So, I tried to see it as any other mother who wants her kid to excel in science because the kid wants to go to med school. Those mothers would be open to their kids staying up late to do homework or study for an exam. I had to let him do that with video games. Like a mom who notices her son's exceptional sports skills and takes him to practices multiple times a week and games on weekends, I too allowed my son to practice and spend his time gaming. This approach led me to take what I later found out was called unschooling. Essentially, this means you learn topics as they present themselves. This unstructured approach made me worry that I was failing my son. I do not stand in front of him at a white board, and he doesn't sit at a desk. He doesn't turn in papers, and I don't give him tests or quizzes. However, when my son took the state's standardized tests, he scored off the charts. Though he was entering 5th grade at the time of testing, he placed into 6th grade English, 5th grade on science and social studies, and 9th grade in math. I was shocked. When I asked my son how he approached the test, he said he "pretended it was a video game." He had played the test like a video game.

The takeaway for me was that I was wrong to worry about failing my son. By allowing his learning to unfold through living and experiencing life, he is thriving. He loves math and because we are free to reimagine learning, he gets to do as much math as he likes, which helps him with gaming. As for the other subjects, we cover them when his interest is sparked, which usually comes from something he has read or seen. When he has a question, we take the time to do the research and learn. I like this method because the information seems to stick a little better since it's something that interests him. In addition, he is developing his ability to find his own answers rather than rely on a teacher to tell him.

My approach to homeschool works for my son. I know my initial feelings of failure came from how I was programmed to think of education. Yet, I had to change for my son's personal well-being. That was more important to me than any grade or social norm I had to force on him. To be clear, homeschooling did not work for my youngest daughter, and it might not work for your child. As parents, we have to get to know our children and then figure out a path we think will work based on their interests.

Song: *"New Slaves"*- Kanye West

Finding Your Path: My Gamer Son Played Your Test , 2021, Acrylic

Part Three

Why you got that attitude?!?

I have been told on multiple occasions that my seven year old daughter has "mad attitude." I actually really hate the word attitude - I'm only using it for context. "Attitude" is a word that society uses to describe the emotions of black women and girls who express passion when speaking. Is having an attitude bad? I don't think so. As you think about that question, consider replacing the word attitude with PASSION. When you replace the statement, "Your daughter has mad attitude" with "Your daughter is mad passionate," it completely changes the nature of her behavior.

Often successful women are passionate about their work and their cause. I see things in their bio, or panel introduction, stating that the presenter is passionate about several things. So, this leads me to believe that passion is accepted, even applauded. What then is the problem with my seven year-old being passionate? It's her age. She is seven, and it's unacceptable to have an attitude per society. Black girls are taught at young ages that their passion is attitude and that, as a child, they must watch their attitude, especially when speaking to adults.

Thankfully, I've been able to see in my daughter what I've been told is attitude, is actually her passion. Understand this: It's not easy to be confronted by a strong-willed, passionate seven year old. Most adults (myself included, at times) don't like the way it feels to be met with what feels like an attitude mostly because it's not the way we grew up. We were told to "respect" adults, but what does that even mean? What I've gathered is this: Don't have an opinion of your own, and if you do have an opinion or idea, keep it to yourself; don't talk back (don't even respond to things being said to/at you); do not defend yourself against anything you're being accused of; do not show emotion of any sort (definitely do not roll your eyes or allow any sounds to come from your mouth); be sure adults are completely finished speaking before you walk away; make sure that your speaking level is at the appropriate decibels at all times and so many more identity-suppressing ideals. So then, what is respect? The protection of the adult's emotions? Control of the child's mind? This is at least what I've discerned the definition to be based on my experience in this society.

I have been trying to make it a practice not to be married to ideas that have been given to me by society. It is not easy. I am a 4o year-old black woman raised in the South. The above-mentioned social constraints regarding "respect" are a part of the training I received in order to be accepted into the society I would one day enter and thrive in. A white society that is afraid of my presence, my attitude, my passion. I had to be tamed so that I would not be too much.

The way I've decided to handle my seven year old daughter's attitude and "disrespectfulness?" I don't handle it at all. Well, at least not in the traditional sense of handling little black girls with attitudes. When I was growing up, I would hear things like, "Who do you think you are with that attitude?"; "Who do you think you are talking to like that?"; "I'm not one of your li'l friends," and "Check your attitude." Hearing these types of statements, I felt coupled to the idea that having an attitude meant my passion was a bad thing. So, my passion was bottled up, and I became a respectable, quiet human. I don't want my seven year-old to lose her passion in the name of shielding an adult from having hurt feelings.

The idea of not suppressing my child's emotion for the sake of others is new for me. I have two older daughters who I didn't allow to express their passion verbally. None of my daughters needed guidance on how to be passionate; they all were born with it. However, my older two, I did attempt to tame. It wasn't until I was around 35 and had gotten years of therapy that I realized, I myself had been tamed. Where did I get my taming you may ask? Society, religion, but most of all the 13 years I spent in public school. Schools train little black and brown children to be "respectful." Stand in line, raise your hand, do not speak unless spoken to, ask permission for anything and everything you do, do not use the restroom until I say you can, don't have an attitude, and many more rules that are designed to control the mind for 13 impressionable years of a human's life. Strange, really, that we as a society put education on such a high pedestal mandating that everyone get an education, then muzzle anyone who uses their brain.

Attitude, also known as passion, is hereditary. It's in our genetic coding. Passion has been at the root of so many successes in the black community. We've been told it's a bad thing by the colonizer, but is it? Or, is it like everything else they tell us about ourselves? It's only negative until they can monetize it, and white people can do it. Rap music, braids, gold chains, and so much more. They told us for years our shit was ghetto -- all of a sudden it's high fashion and every white boy from the suburbs wants to rap. What's next? White girls with attitudes?

Song: *"Nice For What"* - Drake

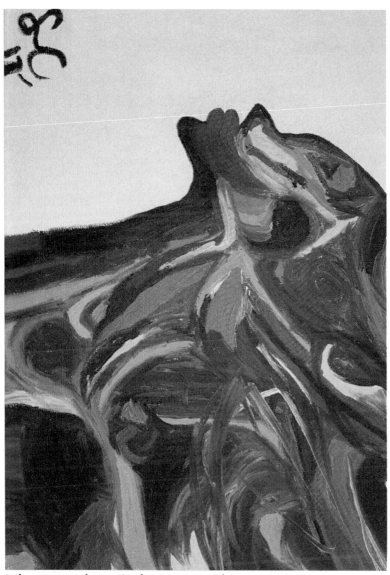

Why you got that attitude ?!?, 2017, Oil

One thing I know, two things for certain

Megan Thee Stallion is good for my daughters.

I like women empowerment. Speak yo mind!

Tell him where to put it.

"I don't like it like that". "I'm not lying to make you happy".

You think I should despise her?

Be mad?

Disgusted?

Are you even a good parent?

You're not a good parent.

[What you need to know about me...I'm from an era where, "boys will be boys", "You were raped because of what you were wearing." "No"means maybe. **Fuck that!**] Male dominated rap fed that narrative.

Sons were never easier to raise than daughters.

You neglected them.

Thank you Megan.

Daughters don't always listen to Moms.

But with a sick beat.

Ass shaking.

Attention seems to be paid.

Freedom is pure space.

Song: *"Girls in the Hood"* - Megan Thee Stallion

One thing I know; two things for certain, 2021, Oil

Wait, Am I doing this right?

To be honest, sometimes I'm scared. Did I do it all wrong? Maybe, I should've been more strict, more demanding. I get frustrated. Ideals have a hold on me. Are they mine? Were they given to me? They were a gift. I should keep them. I think. Naw, they are not mine. Wait, some are.

It's not just me against my thoughts. Often, people decide to share their opinions, solicited or unsolicited. I remember one school counselor telling me that she thought the "problem" she was having with my kid was due to us moving around a lot. She said that I had not created a stable home since we had lived in Texas, Arkansas and now, California. Wow! I think that it taught my kids some amazing skills. Like if you don't like where you are, don't stay. It taught them how to adjust quickly, how to make new friends, how to adjust to new environments, and pay attention to surroundings.

There are moments that I am validated. I put the opinions of others in my back pocket. For instance, my oldest daughter texted me that she's going to move out of her apartment. She no longer wanted to pay rent. She's 23. My default thought was that I have failed. Was the counselor right? The next text was that she's going to Barcelona to live there for a month. Wait, what? Listen. I'm not mad at all, not even a little bit. That counselor was definitely wrong! I am proud. Proud to know she is comfortable traveling the world, exploring. Free of conformity. She does not have a traditional job, and perhaps that's because she was not in a stable home. Opportunities like this do not often present themselves to individuals who chose a more stable/traditional path. People who stand in line, wait their turn, ask permission - aren't free to move, aren't used to being alone, aren't used to change. I realize in these moments that it was not the wrong thing to do. It was just different, which sometimes made it feel wrong. It seems that the humans of society use their personal experience as the measure to construct an idea for society as a whole.

I am not sure why humans exist. Maybe there is no reason. But why not see the world while we are here?

Song: "*Freedom*"- Beyonce

Wait am I doing this Right, 2021, Oil and Acrylic

Just Imagine

Imagine
Leaving traditional school to homeschool your son,
so that he can become a better video game player.

Imagine
Feeling unsure of whether or not you've allowed
too much video gameplay in your home.

Imagine
Encouraging your son to play more video games.

Imagine
Telling your son he hasn't given video gaming the
10,000 hours.

Imagine
Wondering if he sits too long, whether or not
he's physically going to be okay.

Imagine
Thinking if you let him play too long
he will not develop other skills.

Imagine
Him going to visit his grandparents in Arkansas,
where the Internet is not always the best and the possibility
of the game
not working lumes.

Imagine
All the kids in the cul de sac riding bikes and wondering

what will your son be doing?

...

Imagine

He gets on the bike and starts to ride without training.

Imagine

Walking out to see him riding the bike with no hands...

Imagine

Asking him how he did it?

(because he doesn't even own a bike in California)

...

Imagine

His answer is

"I've played video games where I had to ride a bike and that's
how I learned"

...

Imagine

The same kid every time he starts a new outdoor sport; the
coach comes to you and ask "how long has he been playing,
he's so good" and you responding
"today's his first day"

...

Imagine

Listening to society and letting them inform
your decision on what is best for your kids:

Mental health
Physical health
Emotional health
and
Personal well-being

Song: *"Things I Imagined"*- Solange

Just Imagine, 2021, Oil

Wrecking Ball

At a young age, my oldest daughter discovered that she was interested in the sciences. She didn't particularly want to be a doctor but knew she wanted to go to college. Being an academic and a math major, myself, I knew the exact coursework that would be needed. We began to lay the foundation for her future in her sixth grade year. She worked extremely hard (in part because I pushed her to, but she was always down and said it was easy) and rose to the head of her class. Fast forward to her 10th grade year. She had decided that she did not want to attend college in our hometown in Arkansas. She would like to attend a school in California. As a young mom, I did not have a college savings fund for her, so I offered to move to California. This would give her in-state tuition and cut expenses by 50%. I was willing to do this for a couple reasons. She was definitely getting into a college because her transcript was extremely desirable. So, not only would she get into any school she wanted, she would more than likely get scholarships. The other reason was that if we were going to give the state of California that much money every year, we might as well get some enjoyment by living there.

We made the move! The entire family packed up and left for Los Angeles in her 11th grade year of high school (California requires at least one year residency to get in-state tuition). It was difficult. She had been a big fish in a little pond in Arkansas. In LA, she was still a big fish but was now in an ocean with other big fish. The adjustments were hard, but she did it nonetheless. Senior year was stressful with all the college applications, scholarship applications, and finals. I'll never forget; it was super bowl sunday, and we were having a party at our house. She was in her room working on apps when she asked me to help her with one of the questions. I could tell when I walked in that she was completely stressed out. I suggested a break, to come out and have a good time. She just broke down and told me there was no time for that. I took her in my arms, turned her to face me, and told her, "You know you don't have to do this right? Don't do this for me!" She told me that she felt guilty that our whole family had moved here for her to go to college. I assured her that we absolutely love California. We were glad she brought us here and felt the stress she was going through was not necessary for us to feel the worth of being in this state. She stayed in her room and continued her work.

She was accepted to almost all the schools she applied to and chose to attend UCLA. She decided to major in neuroscience.

This is a text exchange we had about mid way through her college career.

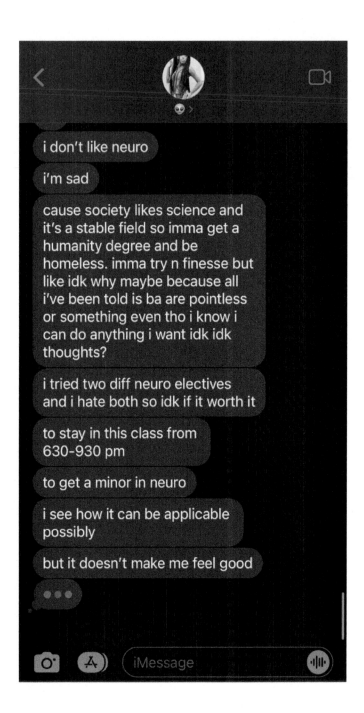

i don't like neuro

i'm sad

cause society likes science and it's a stable field so imma get a humanity degree and be homeless. imma try n finesse but like idk why maybe because all i've been told is ba are pointless or something even tho i know i can do anything i want idk idk thoughts?

i tried two diff neuro electives and i hate both so idk if it worth it

to stay in this class from 630-930 pm

to get a minor in neuro

i see how it can be applicable possibly

but it doesn't make me feel good

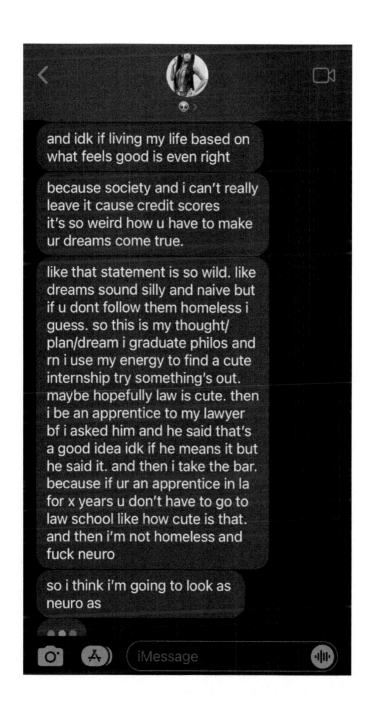

and idk if living my life based on what feels good is even right

because society and i can't really leave it cause credit scores
it's so weird how u have to make ur dreams come true.

like that statement is so wild. like dreams sound silly and naive but if u dont follow them homeless i guess. so this is my thought/plan/dream i graduate philos and rn i use my energy to find a cute internship try something's out. maybe hopefully law is cute. then i be an apprentice to my lawyer bf i asked him and he said that's a good idea idk if he means it but he said it. and then i take the bar. because if ur an apprentice in la for x years u don't have to go to law school like how cute is that. and then i'm not homeless and fuck neuro

so i think i'm going to look as neuro as

iMessage

When you bs on your project but it's your turn to present https://t.co/xLoa1FhnFk

BigDawgJuice 💧
twitter.com

I love you so much girl you are a philosopher Periodt that shit you just said is crazy woke and I only use that word because you black

Delivered

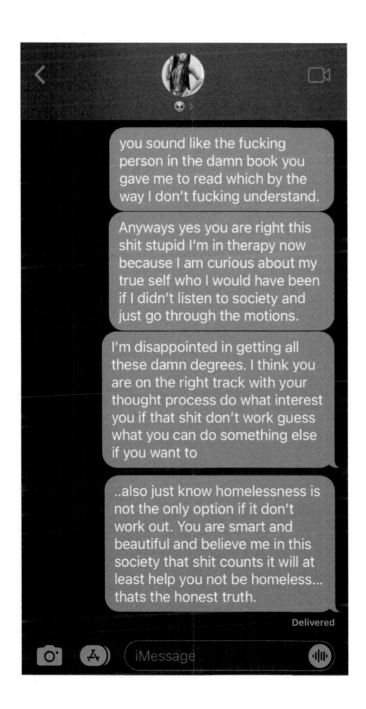

you sound like the fucking person in the damn book you gave me to read which by the way I don't fucking understand.

Anyways yes you are right this shit stupid I'm in therapy now because I am curious about my true self who I would have been if I didn't listen to society and just go through the motions.

I'm disappointed in getting all these damn degrees. I think you are on the right track with your thought process do what interest you if that shit don't work guess what you can do something else if you want to

..also just know homelessness is not the only option if it don't work out. You are smart and beautiful and believe me in this society that shit counts it will at least help you not be homeless... thats the honest truth.

Delivered

iMessage

61

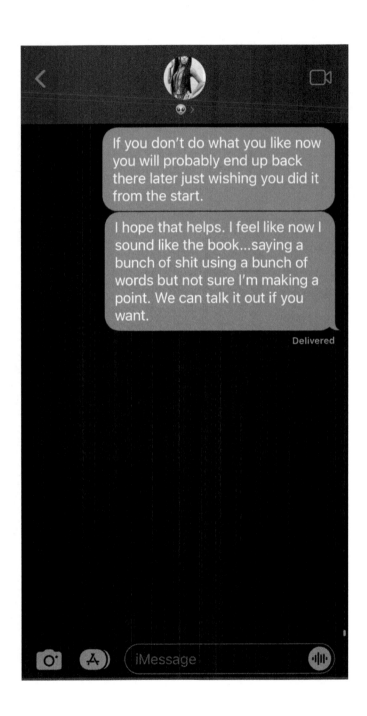

If you don't do what you like now you will probably end up back there later just wishing you did it from the start.

I hope that helps. I feel like now I sound like the book...saying a bunch of shit using a bunch of words but not sure I'm making a point. We can talk it out if you want.

Delivered

She graduated UCLA with a degree in philosophy because it spoke to her soul more than neuroscience...and she listened. She is happy and thriving in her passion of art and thought. She is a painter, a free thinker, a world traveler, and explorer. She designed the cover of this book and has been commissioned for several other artistic projects. I'm so thankful that she didn't have to live a whole lifetime walking in the shoes of someone else's dream for life. I am so proud of her!

The American way of education is like building an unnecessary mansion and then, as soon as you're done, you take a wrecking ball to it only to build a modest home that fits you perfectly. You spend years in k-12 schooling. Sometimes, you spend even more time if you include college. You learn what THEY (society) tell you is important and don't get to spend enough time paying attention to what you think is important. FUCK THEM!

This same society would have had my daughter building an unnecessary mansion (degree in neuroscience) when all she really desired was a modest home (creating art for a living).

Song: *"Phuck U Symphony"*- Millie Jackson

Wrecking Ball, 2015, Oil

What's your name?

"Hi. What's your name?"

Xdfghjklm Nbvcxz.

Wow! That's truly an ugly name.

Why do you have such an ugly name?

Your parents gave you the ugliest name.

No one ever said that to my daughter.

No one ever would.

My middle child doesn't like the name I chose for her.

She has asked us to call her by many different names over her

16 years.

I've accepted the name change each time.

I mean hell, she is the one that has to answer to it.

Write it. Introduce it.

Your name is an important part of your identity.

A name has so much meaning.

A name has no meaning.

It doesn't have to make sense.

Why should it need to make sense to you?

Whose sense is it anyway?

Maybe it's all meaningless.

Oh the freedom in meaninglessness.

The universe seems to be silent on the issue. Society screams.

She should change her name.

I support it.

I feel that this is part of her discovering who she is.

I love and appreciate self discovery.

I wonder if anyone should even be given names at birth.

We should be assigned temporary identifications like:

$j^xg77793^{11}$;

at least until one decides what they want to be called

Song: *"Black & Ugly"*- Raps

What's your name, 2021, Oil

Go see it for yourself

I'm often confused or indifferent ... I can't decide if I should care. Which one? How should I educate my kids? Should I educate my kids? Of course, I should. Right? What should that look like? I don't believe in education. Not as it's currently presented. Try not to misunderstand. I don't want my kids sitting in a classroom listening to a teacher who is supposed to know it all.

Case in point: It's May (school is still in session) and my youngest daughter is currently with her grandmother in Florida on a vacation. Classes have been remote due to the coronavirus pandemic; therefore, I thought it was okay for her to go to Florida. She could take the boring online class with her and do it if she had some free time.

My mom called because she was having a hard time getting her to do any of the work. Our conversation was mostly me explaining how I felt about the matter. Basically, I think it's okay for my daughter not to login and/or do the work. I've sat in those virtual classes, so I've seen what goes on. Nothing. She was in another state and on the other side of the country from where we live. She was witnessing different landscapes, experiencing different climates, cultures, and food. In my opinion, that is the best form of education. As I was saying all this to my mom, she expressed her concern: she wished her mom had pushed her more or harder in terms of pursuing a "good education." Things like making sure that she did her work and studied for tests. I can completely understand the sentiment. However, I must say this is a different time and a different space. My mom lived in a small town in Arkansas, and my daughter lives in a major city in California. Her exposure to things, and the technology that we have in our hands, allow us to learn daily through what we watch, what we listen to, and the people we encounter. I don't think that it's the same thing at all. When my mom was a kid, the closest she would get to knowledge was to go to school and read about it in a book. That is no longer the case. Yet, society still force feeds education through a traditional classroom with outdated books.

I love to learn. I always have. I want my kids to learn and be knowledgeable. I don't like school. School has never provided a space for true evolution. School is box training. It's designed to produce a certain outcome. A nice, controllable, agreeable, respectful, socialized, rule following, unadventurous, conformed human robot.

That's not what I want for my kids. I want them to be kind and thoughtful humans. These traits they learn from home. I want the rest of their education to be through exploration and adventure.

Song: "NICE"- The Carters

Go see for yourself, 2017, Oil

To be or not to be..
Humble

Humble is a hoax; a scam

Like most things American; given to black people.

Be humble; sit down.

Why?

It took a lot for us to get here, why do we need to sit down now when the work we've been doing is finally visible and able to be understood?

Who are we being humble for? Clearly it's not us.

We've been waiting all this time.

Waited...

Until it was the second trimester to even talk about it because:

"The risk of miscarriage usually decreases after the first

trimester."

Carried it for 6 more months.

Doing everything right in hopes that the nurturing would

bring forth fruit that was healthy and beautiful.

The hours of labor are **unspeakable.**

And now we should be **humble?**

Fuck that!

Humble is designed to keep us in a particular space.

I want my kids to be kind and thoughtful.

Not humble.

Song: *"The Blacker the Berry"*- Kendrick Lamar

To be or not to be... Humble, 2021, Acrylic

Humpty Dumpty

Parenting has gotten harder for me. I thought it was supposed to get easier; well, I mean, because the kids are getting older they're more self-sufficient.

I do less for them, but they need me more. They need me different. They need me in a way that I find myself unable to actually help now.

Break-ups with boyfriends/girlfriends/best friends. These things are really hard for me to navigate as a parent because there's really no way I can fix it.

When they were small, I could fix their problems because the problems were typically things you could put your hand on.

Now it's emotional, and I want to fix it, but I can't.

I'd rather have you need me to fix you food than fix your heart.

It saddens me.

Song: "*Ain't No Mountain High Enough*"- Marvin Gaye & Tammi Terrell

Humpty Dumpty, 2021, Oil

I didn't ask to be born.

Parenting has no manual... but, thank god, I love the fact that it doesn't.

Here's why:

There are seven kids in my family and they are all incredibly different. How could one parent guide tell me what to do?

No one can tell you what to do when it comes to your kids. They don't know them, and the truth is, neither do you, at least not fully. You may know what they like to eat or how they respond if upset, but you do not know the ins and outs of their mind just because you are their parent.

Of course, I understand that most parents need or desire some level of guidance. It can be hard and confusing work! I would like to be very clear that I truly believe there is no "right" or "wrong" way to parent.

However, I do believe that parenting should be approached from the perspective of being a resource, not a teacher. I will never forget the day my oldest daughter told me when I was trying to encourage her to work harder, *"I didn't ask to be here."* This was one of the most honest things I have heard as a parent. I never asked any of my children if they wanted to be here, and I brought them into the world anyway, making demands on their presence.

Life is not easy. Society creates and enforces rules, laws, and standards, barely considering the differences in personality among various people. Some of these people didn't ask to be here and may not want to be here, while some accept their own presence and reality. All these types of humans exist in the same space under the same kinds of expectations. This can create all sorts of tension and confusion.

Within this context, parenting from a place where you recognize that these humans didn't ask to come here changes the game. When you tell your child to do or be what you want, you will in all likelihood create friction in your relationship. However, if you stop and remind yourself that this person didn't ask to be here, you may see that this changes what you feel about what you want or are asking of your children and how you interact with them. You become a resource rather than a pedagogue.

Let me give you an example from my own life. With my biological children, I try my best to listen and pay attention to what they do and say. I believe that they tell you and show you who they are from the beginning – the moment they are born. Every one of the kids I birthed have been the same people *from birth*. Birth number 1 was easy – a quiet baby in the nursery. Birth number 2 was more complicated, including food allergies during pregnancy, an early birth, not allowing the full employee benefits to kick in on the new job, and "disturbing the other babies in the nursery" (this is what the nurse said to me the night she brought my baby to me). Birth number 3 was an easy pregnancy with a scheduled c-section. Although birth number 4 was another easy pregnancy, it was followed by distress within days of delivery, ultimately ending in a major surgery. Each one of these experiences are still reflected in each one of my kids who are currently 23, 16, 11, and 8 respectively. The way they came into this world is the way they are in this world. Everything we do after birth as parents and a society is manipulation of this "being." I truly believe that children are not given enough credit for the knowledge they possess from the get-go and the power of their beginning.

We have all been brought into the hierarchy of a society, a hierarchy that tells you that because you've been here on earth longer, you know more. While on some level this is true, it's not absolute. Children come into the world to be as they are. All the molding we attempt to do is unnecessary.

What if we allowed our children space to develop and discover who they are instead of shaping them? What if we stop trying to grow better versions of ourselves? What if we stopped looking for a manual to parent and started being a resource?

People like to judge kids based on their upbringing/parenting. They say things like *"she/he had no home training."* If you are talking about my children, you are damn right skippy. I didn't train them. I don't want carbon copies of myself or my dreams. When you meet one of my children, you will see that they do not pass judgment on what I did or didn't do correctly as a parent. What I did was let them become who they were meant to be, not who I wanted them to be. Who my children are does not and should not be a reflection of me.

Song: *"Ghost Town"*- Kanye West

I didn't ask to be born, 2021, Acrylic

PS

Do you feel frustrated? Yeah, well me too. This book has unresolved issues. I know. This is just my story. There are no definite answers. The answer is in your freedom. Define your freedom. What does that look like to you? What does that mean for your kids? Societal norms. Respectability politics. Unsubscribe. Move forward. It won't fall apart. That's my plan.

Song: *"Changes"*- 2Pac

Playlist

Scan the QR code and enjoy the playlist curated for this book.

Legacy - Jay-Z
Ready or Not - Fugees
A Change is Gonna Come - Sam Cooke
Liberation - Outkast
What's Free - Meek Mill
Neighbors - J. Cole
This Is America - Childish Gambino
I'm Black - Styles P
Mad - Solange
Shelfless - The Clew
New Slaves - Kanye West
Nice For What - Drake
Girls in the Hood - Megan Thee Stallion
Freedom- Beyoncé
Things I Imagined - Solange
Phuck U Symphony - Millie Jackson
Black & Ugly - Rapsody
NICE- The Carters
The Blacker the Berry- Kendrick Lamar
Ain't No Mountain- High Enough
Ghost Town - Kanye West
Changes - 2Pac

Apple Music

Spotify

Printed in Great Britain
by Amazon

81986271R00051